Abraham Lincoln

BY KATY S. DUFFIELD

The Child's World®
childsworld.com

Published by The Child's World®
1980 Lookout Drive • Mankato, MN 56003-1705
800-599-READ • www.childsworld.com

Acknowledgments
The Child's World®: Mary Swensen, Publishing Director
Red Line Editorial: Editorial direction and production
The Design Lab: Design

Photographs ©: Everett Historical/Shutterstock Images,
cover, 1; North Wind Picture Archives, 4; Corbis, 7, 8, 12, 16,
19; Kean Collection/Getty Images, 11; AS400 DB/Corbis, 15;
Bettmann/Corbis, 20

ISBN 9781503808430
LCCN 2015958468

Printed in the United States of America
Mankato, MN
June, 2016
PA02303

ABOUT THE AUTHOR

Katy S. Duffield has a BA in English
from the University of Illinois–
Springfield. She is the author of more
than 20 books for children and has
written both fiction and nonfiction for
many children's magazines.

Table of Contents

Abraham Lincoln did chores as a child.

CHAPTER ONE

A Need to Learn

Twelve-year-old Abraham Lincoln lifted a heavy ax. He swung it over his shoulder. The ax made a dull sound when it hit the wood. Over and over again, Abraham swung.

It was 1821. Abraham and his family lived on a farm in Indiana. Abraham split wood. He built fences. He plowed cornfields and planted seeds. The work never seemed to end.

Abraham was big for his age. So his father counted on him to help out. Abraham did his part.

But what he really wanted to do was learn. He wanted to go to school.

There wasn't much time for school, however. If Abraham wanted to learn, he would have to teach himself. So he did.

Many days, Abraham carried a book with him. He stuffed it into his shirt. At lunch, he laid down his ax. He picked up his book and sat under a shade tree. Abraham ate cornbread. And he read.

At night, Abraham sat beside the fireplace in the cabin. He stretched out his long legs. He worked on math problems.

Abraham practiced writing his letters over and over again. He didn't have a pencil. So he used a piece of charcoal. Or he used a stick to write in the dust, sand, or snow.

Abraham sometimes had to walk for miles to find a book to borrow.

Most of what Abraham learned he taught himself. And his efforts paid off. Abraham Lincoln became one of the most respected men in history.

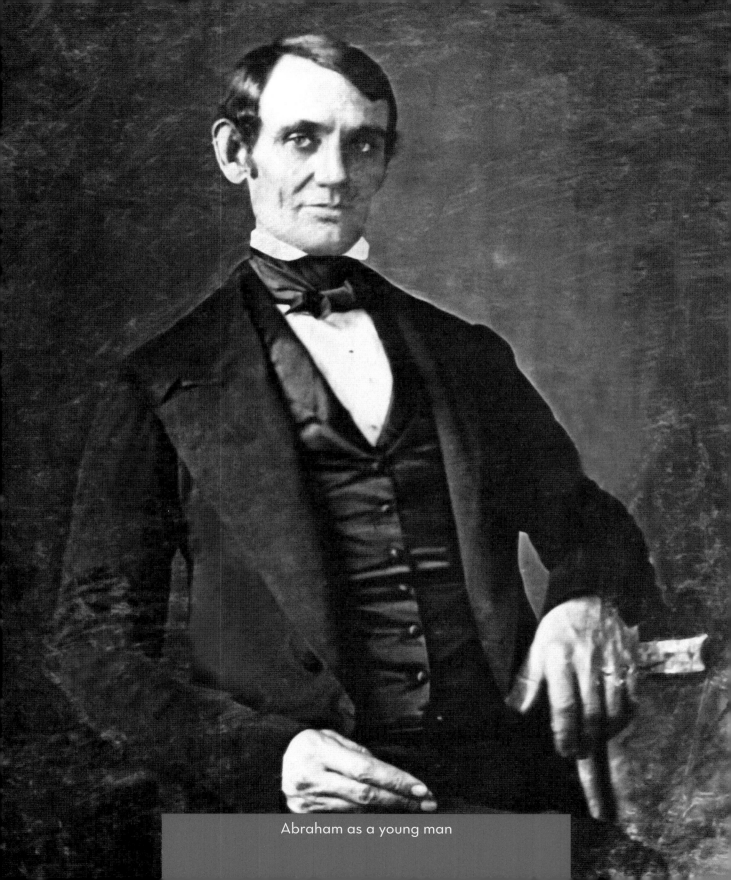

Abraham as a young man

CHAPTER TWO

Abraham's Early Life

On February 12, 1809, Abraham was born in Kentucky. He wasn't born in a hospital. He was born in a tiny log cabin. The cabin had dirt floors. It only had one room.

The Lincoln family was very poor. They had to move from farm to farm. It was the only way they could make a living.

When Abraham was seven, it was time to move again. Abraham and his family went to Indiana. They hoped to find a better farm. But they may have moved for another reason, too. Abraham's father did not want to stay in Kentucky. In Kentucky, it was okay to own **slaves**. Abraham's father thought it was wrong to keep slaves. He did not think one person should own another.

When Abraham was older, he sometimes walked to town. It took a long time to get there. The town was 30 miles (48 km) away. But Abraham didn't mind. He was excited about visiting the **courthouse**. He watched lawyers. He listened to **politicians**. He paid attention to their words. He studied their actions.

Abraham thought he'd like to make a **speech**. So he started practicing. He didn't practice on people, though. He gave his speech to trees and to cornstalks.

Soon, Abraham was ready. He stood in front of a store in Illinois. He gave his first speech.

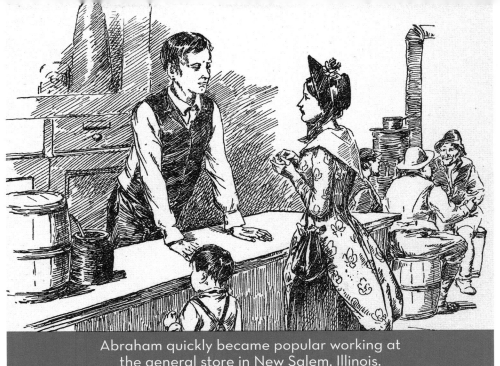

Abraham quickly became popular working at the general store in New Salem, Illinois.

Abraham left home when he was 22. He moved to a town in Illinois. It was called New Salem. Abraham worked as a **clerk** in the village store. He met a lot of people. He made many friends.

Abraham liked working at the store. But he didn't want to be a clerk forever. He didn't want to be a farmer like his father either. Abraham was getting older. It was time for him to think about what he was going to do with his life.

Lincoln studied in his log cabin.

CHAPTER THREE

Becoming a Leader

Abraham Lincoln thought he might like to be a politician. He thought being a lawyer might be a good job, too. For those jobs, he needed to speak and write well. So Lincoln borrowed an English grammar book. He spent a lot of time studying it. Then, Lincoln had his friends test him. He wanted to see what he had learned.

Lincoln made a plan in 1832. He wanted to be a **lawmaker** for Illinois. Lincoln gave speeches. He shared his ideas.

Soon, it was election day. People voted. Lincoln didn't win. But he did get a lot of votes. Almost everyone in New Salem voted for him.

Lincoln did not like losing. But he was young. He would have other chances. Lincoln knew what he needed. He needed to be more prepared.

In two years, Lincoln ran again. This time, he won. Lincoln became a state lawmaker.

Lincoln moved to Springfield, Illinois. He met with other lawmakers. They talked. They argued. They shared ideas. Lincoln did not say much at first. He mostly watched and learned. But soon, he became more sure of himself. It became easier for him to share his views.

Lincoln worked hard. He was a lawmaker for eight years. He also kept studying law. In 1836, he became a lawyer.

Lincoln was called "Honest Abe" when he was a lawyer.

A few years later, Lincoln got a new job. He was elected to the United States Congress. Lincoln wanted to pass an important law. He wanted it to be **illegal** to own slaves. It was his first try to stop people from keeping slaves. But his law did not pass. Lincoln did not give up. He thought owning slaves was wrong.

During his run for the presidency, Lincoln participated in several debates with his opponent Stephen Douglas.

CHAPTER FOUR

Our 16th President

Lincoln became a successful congressman. He was widely known for his opinion on slavery. Many people liked him. This led Lincoln to become the Republican Party pick for president. In 1860, Lincoln ran for president of the United States. He won.

The country had many problems at that time. One of the biggest problems was slavery. Many people from the South wanted to keep slaves. Most from the North thought slavery was wrong.

The North and the South argued about something else, too. The South no longer wanted to be a part of the United States. They wanted to make their own laws. They were worried that slavery would be made illegal. These **disagreements** caused a war. It was called the Civil War.

Lincoln felt that the states should stay together. He was against keeping slaves.

So Lincoln fought for what he believed in. In 1863, he wrote an important paper. It was called the Emancipation Proclamation. It ordered all slaves in the South to be set free. Later that year, he made a famous speech. It was called the Gettysburg Address. Lincoln's words honored those who had died in the Civil War. He talked about working together. He said that all people should be free.

Many people lost their lives in the war. It dragged on for four years. It was one of the worst times in U.S. history.

The Battle of Gettysburg in July 1863

The assassination of President Abraham Lincoln in Ford's Theater

The war came to an end in 1865. The North
won. Lincoln's work had paid off. Keeping slaves was
against the law. The states were **united** once again.

The war was over. But many people were still angry. They did not like that Lincoln had helped **abolish** slavery.

On April 14, 1865, an angry man followed Lincoln. His name was John Wilkes Booth. He came up behind Lincoln in a theater. Booth pulled a gun and shot the president. Lincoln died the next morning. He was 56 years old.

People have never forgotten Abraham Lincoln. He was an important man and an important president. He never stopped learning. He never stopped working to keep the United States together. He never stopped working to make people free.

1800

← **February 12, 1809** Abraham Lincoln is born in Kentucky.

← **1816** The Lincoln family moves to Indiana.

← **1830** Lincoln makes his first speech.

← **1831** Lincoln leaves his family and moves to New Salem, Illinois.

← **1832** Lincoln enters his first political race but does not win.

← **1834** Lincoln begins studying law.

← **August 4, 1834** Lincoln wins his first election and begins serving as an Illinois lawmaker.

← **1836** Lincoln becomes a lawyer.

← **August 3, 1846** Lincoln is elected to the U.S. Congress.

← **November 6, 1860** Lincoln is elected the 16th president of the United States.

← **January 1, 1863** Lincoln signs the Emancipation Proclamation that gives freedom to slaves.

← **November 19, 1863** Lincoln makes a famous speech called the Gettysburg Address.

← **April 14, 1865** Lincoln is shot.

← **April 15, 1865** Lincoln dies from the gunshot wound.

1870

abolish (ah-BAL-ish) Abolish means put an end to something. Lincoln wanted to abolish slavery.

clerk (KLERK) A clerk is a person who keeps records. Lincoln worked as a clerk when he moved to New Salem, Illinois.

courthouse (KORT-howse) A courthouse is a building where legal cases are heard. Lincoln walked to a courthouse to watch lawyers work.

disagreements (dis-uh-GREE-ments) Disagreements are when people argue because they have different views on something. Disagreements between Northern and Southern states caused the Civil War.

illegal (ih-LEE-guhl) If something is illegal, it is not allowed by the law. Lincoln wanted to make it illegal to own slaves.

lawmaker (LAW-may-ker) A lawmaker is a person who makes rules or laws that people must follow. After he was elected, Lincoln and other lawmakers met in Springfield.

politicians (pahl-ih-TISH-uhns) Politicians are people who are elected to work in government. When he was a young man, Lincoln admired politicians.

slaves (SLAVES) Slaves are people who are owned and controlled by another person. Lincoln thought it was wrong to own slaves.

speech (SPEECH) A speech is a talk given to an audience. The Gettysburg Address is Lincoln's most famous speech.

united (yoo-NI-ted) If two or more things are united, they have come together as one. At the end of the Civil War, the North and South were united.

In the Library

Gilpin, Caroline Crosson. *Abraham Lincoln*. Washington, DC: National Geographic Children's Books, 2012.

Krull, Kathleen and Paul Brewer. *Lincoln Tells a Joke: How Laughter Saved the President (and the Country)*. New York: Harcourt Children's Books, 2010.

Thomson, Sarah L. *What Lincoln Said*. New York: HarperCollins Publishers, 2009.

On the Web

Visit our Web site for links about
Abraham Lincoln: **childsworld.com/links**

Note to Parents, Teachers, and Librarians: We routinely verify our Web links to make sure they are safe and active sites. So encourage your readers to check them out!

INDEX